Service Provider's Manual

Practices of Excellence to Turn Clients into Fans

Paulo Ehms

MMXXIV

Copyright Notice © 2024 Paulo Ehms

All rights reserved. No part of this book may be reproduced, stored, or transmitted in any form or by any means, electronic or mechanical, including photocopying, recording, or by any information storage and retrieval system, without written permission from the copyright holder, except for brief quotations embedded in critical reviews and other uses permitted by copyright law.

For permission requests, please contact:
pauloehms@hotmail.com

Table of Contents

Introduction 5
   Exploring the World of Service Providers 5
Chapter 1 7
   Unraveling the World of Service Providers 7
   Importance of the Service Provider Manual 9
Chapter 2 12
   Profile of the Service Provider 12
   Necessary Skills 14
   Profile of the Service Provider 16
Chapter 3 20
   Preparation 20
   Relevant Certifications 22
   Portfolio 24
Chapter 4 28
   Establishing Your Business 28
   Records and Licenses 30
   Financial Planning 33
Chapter 5 36
   Personal Branding 36
   Marketing Strategies 38
   Utilization of Social Media 41
Chapter 6 44
   Customer Management 44
   Communication 47
   Conflict Resolution 49

Chapter 7 52
   Service Delivery 52
   Project Management 55
   Quality Customer Service 57

Chapter 8 61
   Legal and Contractual Aspects 61
   Rights and Duties 64
   Dispute Resolution 67

Chapter 9 70
   Useful Tools and Resources 70
   Marketing Platforms 73
   Networking 75

Chapter 10 79
   Continuous Professional Development 79
   Continuing Education 82
   Adaptation to Changes 85

Chapter 11 89
   Case Studies 89

Chapter 12 93
   Ethics in Service Delivery and Its Contribution to Building a Lasting Reputation 93
   The Importance of a "Good Name" 96

Conclusion 99
   Recap of Key Points 99
   Encouragement for Continuous Success 102
   Recommended Books for Additional Resources 105

Introduction

Exploring the World of Service Providers

Welcome to the "Service Provider Manual"! This book has been carefully crafted to guide you through the fascinating universe of entrepreneurship and service provision. Whether you're an experienced service provider or just beginning to consider this journey, this guide will provide valuable insights, practical tips, and fundamental guidance for your success.

In a dynamic and increasingly competitive landscape, service provision emerges as a promising path for freelancers and entrepreneurs. Whether you're a graphic designer, programmer, consultant, or any other profession, this manual will offer a comprehensive roadmap, covering everything from building your skills to effectively managing your own business.

In Chapter 1, we will take the first steps, contextualizing the importance of this manual and highlighting how it will become a valuable tool in your journey. Throughout the pages, we'll explore crucial topics such as defining the ideal service provider profile, preparing to face challenges, and structuring your own business.

From here, we'll embark on a journey of learning and improvement, addressing practical aspects such as contract drafting and client management, to building an effective online presence and strategies to stand out in the market.

Be prepared to discover useful tools and resources that will optimize your productivity and efficiency, as well as learn from inspiring case studies of successful service providers.

As you conclude this journey, we hope you feel empowered and inspired to reach new heights in your career as a service provider. Get ready to explore this exciting path full of challenges, achievements, and professional growth. Success awaits you, and this manual is your reliable guide on this thrilling journey!

Chapter 1

Unraveling the World of Service Providers

Welcome to the heart of this guide, where we will unravel together the intricate world of service providers. This initial chapter serves as a gateway to a journey filled with discoveries, learnings, and above all, opportunities for your professional growth.

1.1 Why This Book?

Discover the Purpose: As we launch this book, our primary objective is to provide you with a reliable compass amidst the vast territory of service provision. The complexity of the current landscape demands a strategic approach, and this guide is designed to be your compass, guiding you through every challenge, every decision, and every moment of growth.

1.2 What to Expect?

Roadmap to Success: Throughout the following sections, we will explore the essential fundamentals that comprise the service provider's journey. From defining the ideal profile to client management, each topic has been carefully selected to empower you to navigate the often turbulent waters of this sector, providing you with the necessary tools to build a solid and successful career.

1.3 Who Is This Book For?

A Universal Guide: This book is intended for a wide range of professionals, from those taking their first steps in service provision to the most experienced entrepreneurs. Whether you're a designer, consultant, writer, or professional from any field, the information contained here is adaptable and relevant to all service providers seeking to stand out in the market.

1.4 How to Use This Guide? N

avigating Through the Pages: Throughout this manual, you'll find practical tips, real-world examples, and exercises that will challenge you to apply the knowledge gained. We suggest reading sequentially, but feel free to explore sections according to your specific needs.

We are excited to begin this journey with you. Let's dive together into the pages of the "Service Provider Manual" and unravel the strategies that will drive your success in this dynamic and challenging world. The journey begins now!

Importance of the Service Provider Manual

1.2 Importance of the Service Provider Manual

The world of service provision is vast, dynamic, and sometimes challenging. In this context, the question arises: why is a specific manual for service providers so crucial? The answer lies in the understanding that proper preparation and solid knowledge are indispensable foundations for building a successful career. Let's explore the fundamental importance of this guide and how it becomes an indispensable tool for the modern service provider.

1.2.1 Strategic Guidance

Navigate with Confidence: When entering the world of service provision, it's easy to feel lost amidst the many options, challenges, and decisions. This manual provides strategic guidance, helping you chart a clear path and make informed decisions. Having a comprehensive view of the essential fundamentals will empower you to act with confidence and determination.

1.2.2 Overcoming Obstacles

Anticipate Challenges: Service provision presents a series of challenges, from fierce competition to complex legal issues. The manual tackles these obstacles head-on, offering insights and strategies to anticipate and overcome common challenges. Being prepared for adversities is key to avoiding pitfalls and staying resilient.

1.2.3 Building Solid Foundations

Create a Lasting Career: To build a solid career, it's essential to have strong foundations. This manual provides practical information and a framework for continuous development. Learning the fundamentals from the beginning is like building sturdy foundations, ensuring that your career grows sustainably over time.

1.2.4 Adaptation to Changes

Stay Updated: The business world and service provision are constantly evolving. In addition to addressing current practices, the manual offers insights on how to adapt to changes in the market. The ability to stay relevant and innovative is a significant advantage, and this guide prepares you to face future challenges.

1.2.5 Empowerment of the Professional

Turn Knowledge into Power: By understanding the importance of this manual, you empower yourself with knowledge that transcends theory. The goal is to empower you to make informed decisions, take control of your career, and turn knowledge into power. This guide is a dynamic tool for building your success.

Understanding the significance of this manual, you'll be ready to dive into the subsequent sections, prepared to absorb the insights, strategies, and practical guidance that will guide you in building a successful service provision career. The journey is just beginning, and you're in control.

Chapter 2

Profile of the Service Provider

2.1 Essential Qualities

To successfully navigate the path of service provision, it is crucial to develop and enhance certain essential qualities that shape your professional identity and determine the level of excellence you can achieve in your endeavors. Let's explore some of the fundamental qualities that characterize a successful service provider.

2.1.1 Professionalism

Commitment to Ethics:

Being a service provider entails representing not only yourself but also the ethical values of your work. Professionalism goes beyond technical skills; it involves meeting deadlines, communicating effectively, and treating clients and colleagues with respect. It is the foundation upon which solid professional relationships are built.

2.1.2 Empathy

Understanding the Customer: Understanding the needs and expectations of customers is an essential skill. Empathy allows you to put yourself in the customer's shoes, understanding their concerns and desires. This quality strengthens the professional relationship and guides the delivery of personalized and high-quality services.

2.1.3 Effective Communication

Clear Transmission of Ideas: The ability to communicate clearly and effectively is a significant advantage. From crafting proposals to daily interaction with clients, communication is the backbone of service provision. Developing this skill enhances mutual understanding and avoids misunderstandings that may arise during the process.

2.1.4 Proactivity

Anticipation of Needs: Being proactive means anticipating the client's needs and taking the initiative to solve problems. In a service provision environment, proactivity highlights the professional, demonstrating commitment and dedication to exceeding the client's expectations.

2.1.5 Problem-Solving Skills

Dealing with Challenges: Challenges are inevitable in service provision. Having the ability to identify problems, analyze solutions, and implement corrective actions is vital. Effective problem-solving demonstrates your competence and builds trust with both clients and other professionals in the industry.

2.1.6 Adaptability

Flexibility for Changes: The service provision environment is subject to rapid changes. Being able to adapt to new circumstances, technologies, and market demands is a valuable quality.

Adaptability ensures that you remain relevant and competitive over time.

By developing and incorporating these essential qualities into your professional approach, you will be building the foundations for a solid career in service provision. In the next topic, we will address the importance of continuous development and education to further enhance your skills.

Necessary Skills

2.2 Necessary Skills

In addition to personal qualities, service provision demands a specific set of technical skills that empower the professional to deliver quality services and stand out in their field of expertise. Let's explore the essential skills that are crucial for success as a service provider.

2.2.1 Technical Specialization

Master of Your Craft: Regardless of the sector you operate in, technical specialization is a fundamental requirement. Delving deep into your specific skills, whether it's programming, design, consulting, or any other area, enhances your efficiency and establishes you as a reference in your field.

2.2.2 Project Management

Efficient Deliveries: The ability to manage projects efficiently is crucial in service provision. From setting goals to allocating resources and meeting deadlines, project management ensures that you deliver high-quality services in an organized and professional manner.

2.2.3 Financial Knowledge

Personal and Business Financial Management: Understanding basic financial principles is essential. This includes the ability to create budgets, price your services appropriately, and manage your business finances effectively. Solid financial skills ensure the long-term sustainability of your operations.

2.2.4 Negotiation Skills

Alignment of Interests: Negotiation is an art, especially in service provision. The ability to negotiate contractual terms, prices, and expectations with clients, partners, and suppliers is vital to ensure healthy relationships and mutually beneficial agreements.

2.2.5 Analytical Thinking

Data-Driven Decision Making: Analyzing data and information is crucial for making informed decisions. Analytical thinking empowers the service provider to evaluate situations, identify trends, and adjust strategies to better meet market needs.

2.2.6 Personal Marketing

Effective Promotion: Knowing how to promote your services is as important as the quality of the work itself. Developing personal marketing skills, whether online or offline, helps create a prominent presence in the market, attracting new clients and opportunities.

2.2.7 Technological Competencies

Keeping Up with Innovations: We live in an ever-evolving digital age. Staying updated with the latest technologies and tools in your field enhances your efficiency and demonstrates a commitment to innovation and excellence.

By incorporating these technical skills into your professional arsenal, you will be better prepared to face challenges and excel in service provision.

Profile of the Service Provider

2.3 Types of Service Providers

The diversity in the field of service provision is remarkable, encompassing a wide range of professionals, each with their specialties and unique approaches. In this topic, we will explore some of the most common types of service providers, recognizing the variety of skills and talents that contribute to the richness of this dynamic sector.

2.3.1 Consultants

Solution Specialists: Consultants are experts in their fields, offering valuable insights and strategies to help companies and individuals overcome specific challenges. Their analytical and problem-solving skills are essential for guiding strategic decisions.

2.3.2 Freelancers

Professional Independence: Freelancers are self-employed professionals who offer their services in various areas such as writing, design, programming, among others. Their autonomy allows flexibility, although efficient time management and continuous pursuit of opportunities are crucial.

2.3.3 Service Entrepreneurs

Business Creation and Management: These are service providers who offer their skills and often manage complete businesses. They take on financial responsibilities, lead teams, and often develop innovative solutions to meet market demands.

2.3.4 Health and Wellness Professionals

Caring for Body and Mind: Including doctors, therapists, personal trainers, and others, these service providers focus on the health and well-being of clients. Their skills go beyond technical expertise, involving empathy and a holistic understanding of the client.

2.3.5 Technology Specialists

Innovation and Development: Technology professionals, such as software developers, engineers, and cybersecurity experts, play a crucial role in the digital age. Their skills are essential for the constant evolution of the technological landscape.

2.3.6 Marketing Service Providers

Promoting and Positioning Brands: Specializing in marketing strategies, these professionals help companies increase their visibility, attract clients, and position their brands in the market. Their skills range from digital marketing to traditional advertising strategies.

2.3.7 Creative Service Providers

Expressing Art and Design: Artists, designers, writers, and musicians make up this group, contributing creativity to various sectors. Their artistic skills are essential for visual and conceptual communication in a variety of projects.

2.3.8 Education Professionals

Knowledge Transmission: Educators and trainers are service providers dedicated to the transmission of knowledge and skills. Whether in classrooms, online, or in corporate training, they play a vital role in the development of individual and organizational capabilities.

By understanding the diversity of service provider types, you can identify where your skills and interests fit best, directing your career more effectively. In the next chapter, we will discuss the necessary preparation to navigate this path with confidence and success.

Chapter 3

Preparation

3.1 Education and Training

The solid foundation for a successful career in service provision largely rests on the constant pursuit of knowledge and continuous development. In this first topic, we will explore the importance of formal education and specific training as fundamental elements for the preparation and enhancement of the service provider.

3.1.1 Formal Education

The Power of Academic Knowledge: Formal education, such as degrees, certifications, and university courses, provides a solid theoretical foundation for professional practice. This academic knowledge validates your skills but also provides a comprehensive understanding of fundamental principles in your field of expertise.

3.1.2 Specific Courses

Skill-Focused Training: In addition to formal education, specific courses tailored to your area of specialization provide practical and updated learning. These courses are often designed to meet market demands, providing specific skills ready to be applied in the professional environment.

3.1.3 Workshops and Seminars

Interactive Learning: Participating in workshops and seminars provides a hands-on and interactive experience. These events allow for the exchange of ideas, networking with other professionals, and access to recent information and trends in your field, significantly contributing to continuous improvement.

3.1.4 Professional Certifications

Validation of Competencies: Professional certifications are industry-recognized seals of approval, validating your specific competencies. They undoubtedly add credibility to your profile, but more importantly, demonstrate a commitment to excellence and compliance with recognized standards.

3.1.5 Continuing Education

Ongoing Investment in Knowledge: Service provision is a dynamic field, subject to rapid changes and constant innovations. Continuing education, whether through online courses, relevant readings, or participation in webinars, ensures that you are always up-to-date and ready to face the evolving challenges in your industry.

3.1.6 Development of Social Skills

Beyond the Technical: In addition to technical skills, the development of social skills such as effective communication, empathy, and collaboration is crucial. Many aspects of service provision involve interpersonal interactions, and enhancing these skills contributes to stronger professional relationships.

By investing time and effort in your education and training, you not only strengthen your technical skills but also position yourself as a professional dedicated to continuous improvement. In the next topic, we will explore the importance of obtaining relevant certifications as an integral part of your journey in service provision.

Relevant Certifications

3.2 Relevant Certifications

In a world where competition is fierce and skills validation is crucial, professional certifications play a significant role in the service provider's journey. In this topic, we will explore the importance of obtaining relevant certifications, highlighting how these seals of approval can boost your credibility and open doors to valuable opportunities.

3.2.1 Recognition of Competence

External Validation: Relevant certifications not only validate your skills but also provide external recognition of your competence in a specific area.

This is particularly crucial in a market where client trust is essential.

3.2.2 Market Differentiation

Stand Out from the Competition: In a competitive landscape, certifications offer a tangible way to distinguish yourself from the competition. Employers and clients often seek professionals who have demonstrated commitment to acquiring knowledge and improving their skills.

3.2.3 Access to Specific Opportunities

Certifications Open Doors: Relevant certifications often open doors to specific job opportunities or projects. Some companies and clients value specific certifications when seeking service providers for specialized roles.

3.2.4 Continuous Updating

Keeping Up with Industry Trends: Many certifications require the completion of courses or periodic exams to maintain validity. This encourages continuous updating and keeps you aligned with the latest trends and practices in your field.

3.2.5 Building Confidence

Quality Assurance: For clients and employers, certifications are often seen as assurances of quality. They offer a clear indication that you possess the skills and knowledge necessary to perform at a high level.

3.2.6 Professional Growth

Career Progression: Certifications can be a stepping stone for professional growth. They solidify your current position and can open up opportunities for more advanced and challenging roles over time.

3.2.7 Conscious Choice of Certifications

Alignment with Your Goals: When pursuing certifications, it is crucial to choose those that align directly with your professional goals. Relevant certifications enhance your credibility when they resonate with your specialization and career objectives.

By investing in relevant certifications, you strengthen your knowledge base and build a more attractive professional profile. In the next topic, we will address the construction and importance of a solid portfolio to highlight your accomplishments and competencies.

Portfolio

3.3 Building a Portfolio

In addition to certifications and formal education, one of the most powerful elements to showcase your skills and experiences is creating a robust portfolio. In this topic, we will explore the importance of a well-crafted portfolio and how this essential tool can be the key to winning clients, employers, and significant opportunities.

3.3.1 What is a Portfolio?

A Showcase of Your Achievements: A portfolio is more than just a simple collection of past works. It is a dynamic showcase that highlights your skills, experiences, and accomplishments. It serves as a virtual storefront that allows interested parties to assess your work and understand your professional approach.

3.3.2 Importance of Portfolio in Service Provision

Practical Demonstration of Skills: While certifications and diplomas validate your theoretical skills, a portfolio offers a practical demonstration of your knowledge. Clients and employers often want to see concrete examples of your work before making decisions.

3.3.3 Essential Elements of the Portfolio

Variety and Quality: An effective portfolio should include a variety of works that represent your skills comprehensively. Make sure to include projects that highlight different aspects of your competencies and demonstrate your ability to adapt.

3.3.4 Organized Structure

Intuitive Navigation: Organize your portfolio logically and intuitively. Categorize your works, provide a brief description of each project, and highlight the challenges faced and solutions applied. Make it easy for visitors to find and understand your work.

3.3.5 Detailed Case Studies

Contextualization and Creative Process: Include detailed case studies for key projects. This not only provides context about the work but also reveals your creative process, decision-making, and analytical skills.

3.3.6 Feedback and Testimonials

External Validation: Incorporate testimonials and feedback from previous clients. These recommendations provide external validation of your work and contribute to building trust with future clients or employers.

3.3.7 Continuous Updating

Reflection of Professional Growth: Keep your portfolio updated as you progress in your career. New projects, certifications, and experiences should be added to reflect your continuous professional growth.

3.3.8 Online Portfolio

Easy and Global Access: Having an online portfolio is essential in the digital age. This allows potential clients or employers to easily access your work from anywhere in the world. Consider creating a website or using dedicated platforms to host your portfolio.

By creating a portfolio that highlights not only your technical skills but also your approach and practical experiences, you build a powerful tool to seize opportunities in service provision. In the next chapter, we will explore the intricate journey of establishing your own business in service provision.

Chapter 4

Establishing Your Business

4.1 Legal Structures for Small Businesses

When embarking on the journey of establishing your own business in the United States, choosing the legal structure is one of the most crucial decisions. Each legal structure has significant implications for the organization of the business, legal, and tax responsibilities. Let's explore some of the common legal structures for small businesses.

4.1.1 Sole Proprietorship

Autonomy and Simplicity: Sole Proprietorship is an option for those who wish to start a business in a simple and straightforward manner. In this structure, the owner is solely responsible for the business, offering autonomy but also implying unlimited liability for debts and obligations.

4.1.2 Partnership

Collaboration and Sharing: Partnership allows two or more people to share responsibility for managing and operating the business. Profits and losses are divided among partners according to the terms of the partnership agreement.

4.1.3 Limited Liability Company (LLC)

Liability Limitation: LLC provides owners with protection against personal liability for business debts and obligations. It is a flexible structure that combines aspects of partnerships and corporations, offering tax and organizational benefits.

4.1.4 Corporation

Separate Legal Entity: A Corporation is a legal entity separate from its owners, meaning it can be held liable for its own debts and legal obligations. There are different types of corporations, such as S-Corporations and C-Corporations, each with its own characteristics and tax requirements.

4.1.5 Nonprofit Corporation

Social or Charitable Purpose: A Nonprofit Corporation is an entity organized to achieve charitable, educational, religious, scientific, among other purposes, and does not distribute profits to its members or directors. It offers tax benefits for donors and may seek grants and specific funding.

4.1.6 Conscious Choice and Professional Consultation

The Importance of Legal Guidance: Choosing the legal structure should be a conscious and informed decision. It is highly recommended to seek legal guidance to understand the specific implications of each option, considering the characteristics of your business, goals, and current legal context.

4.1.7 Tax and Accounting Aspects

Tax and Accounting Planning: In addition to legal implications, consider the tax and accounting aspects of each legal structure. Properly planning these aspects from the outset is essential to ensure compliance and optimize the tax efficiency of your business.

By understanding the different legal structures available in the United States, you can make an informed decision that aligns with your specific needs and goals.

Records and Licenses

4.2 Registration and Necessary Licenses

In addition to choosing the appropriate legal form, registering and obtaining the necessary licenses are crucial steps in establishing your service business. These processes ensure the legality of operations, establish the basis for transparent business relationships, and demonstrate a commitment to regulatory compliance. Let's explore these essential elements.

4.2.1 Registration with the Secretary of State

Business Formalization: Registering with the Secretary of State is a fundamental step in formalizing your business. This process establishes the legal existence of the company, provides an EIN (Employer Identification Number), and allows for the issuance of invoices.

4.2.2 Municipal Registration

Local Compliance: Municipal registration is necessary for the business to comply with specific municipal regulations. This may involve obtaining a business license and complying with local zoning regulations.

4.2.3 Sectoral Licenses

Meeting Specific Requirements: In some service areas, specific sectoral licenses may be required. This applies to regulated sectors such as healthcare, law, accounting, and others, where legislation requires additional certifications or authorizations.

4.2.4 Environmental Licenses

Attention to Sustainability: Depending on the nature of the service, environmental permits may be required to ensure compliance with regulations related to environmental issues and sustainability.

4.2.5 Trademark and Patent Registration

Intellectual Property Protection: If your service provision involves the creation of unique products, brands, or processes, trademark and patent registration is essential to protect your intellectual property and avoid potential legal conflicts.

4.2.6 Business Insurance

Protection against Risks: Obtaining business insurance is a wise measure to protect the business against various risks, such as liability, property damage, and other unforeseen events that may arise during operations.

4.2.7 Compliance with Labor Standards

Transparent Labor Relations: If employees are hired, it is crucial to comply with labor standards, maintain proper records, provide safe working conditions, and comply with laws related to wages and benefits.

4.2.8 Consultation with Specialized Professionals

Legal and Accounting Guidance: Given the complexity and variability of regulations, it is highly recommended to seek guidance from specialized professionals, such as lawyers and accountants, to ensure that all legal requirements are met adequately.

By registering and obtaining the necessary licenses, you establish the foundation for a solid business that complies with applicable laws and regulations.

Financial Planning

4.3 Initial Financial Planning

The success of a service-based business often hinges on solid financial management from the outset. Initial financial planning is crucial to avoid unpleasant surprises, ensure the sustainability of the venture, and provide a solid foundation for growth. In this topic, we will explore the key aspects of initial financial planning.

4.3.1 Budget Development

Estimates and Projections: Start financial planning by developing a detailed budget. Estimate monthly revenues and expenses, taking into account all operational costs, salaries, marketing, and other business-related expenses.

4.3.2 Initial Capital and Investment

Assessment of Needs: Identify the amount of initial capital required to start operations. Consider investments in equipment, marketing, training, and any other initial expenses. Ensuring adequate investment is crucial to support the business in its early stages.

4.3.3 Emergency Reserve

Preparation for Contingencies: Establish an emergency reserve to deal with unforeseen events. This reserve provides a financial safety net, allowing the business to overcome temporary challenges without compromising operations.

4.3.4 Cost Control

Operational Efficiency: Rigorously control operational costs. Evaluate the feasibility of cutting non-essential expenses and look for ways to streamline processes to ensure operational efficiency.

4.3.5 Proper Pricing

Balance between Value and Competitiveness: Set prices that not only cover costs but also provide profit. Consider competitive pricing, but ensure that the prices charged align with the value perceived by customers.

4.3.6 Cash Flow

Efficient Management: Monitor cash flow closely. Good cash flow management is vital to ensure that the company has the necessary resources to operate daily and meet its financial obligations.

4.3.7 Payment Strategies

Clear Terms with Customers and Suppliers: Establish clear payment terms with customers and suppliers. This includes billing policies, payment deadlines, and strategies for dealing with delinquency, ensuring balanced financial health.

4.3.8 Tax Planning

Responsible Tax Optimization: Consult with an accountant to develop an effective tax plan. Tax planning can help optimize the business's tax burden, ensuring compliance and maximizing available tax benefits.

4.3.9 Periodic Review

Adapting to Changes: Financial planning is not a static process. Conduct periodic reviews to assess financial performance, adjust projections and strategies as necessary, and ensure that the business remains resilient to environmental changes.

By prioritizing initial financial planning, you will be laying the groundwork for a solid and sustainable service-based business. In the next chapter, we will explore marketing and promotional strategies, essential for attracting clients and expanding your business's visibility.

Chapter 5

Personal Branding

5.1 Building the Initial Personal Brand

Building a personal brand is a fundamental piece of the puzzle for success in service provision. Your personal brand is not just a representation of what you do but also an authentic expression of who you are as a professional. In this first topic, we will explore strategies for building a solid and authentic initial personal brand.

5.1.1 Self-awareness and Professional Identity

Reflection on Skills and Values: Before you begin building your personal brand, it's crucial to deeply reflect on your skills, values, and professional goals. Identify what makes you unique and which aspects of your personality can be highlighted to create an authentic connection with your target audience.

5.1.2 Goal Definition

Clear and Measurable Goals: Set clear goals for your personal brand. These objectives may include acquiring certain clients, entering a specific market, or being recognized as an expert in your field. Well-defined goals will guide your brand-building strategies.

5.1.3 Visual Identity

Consistency and Professionalism: Visual identity is a vital part of brand building. Develop a logo and use consistent colors and fonts in your marketing materials, resume, and online presence. A cohesive visual identity conveys professionalism and aids in brand memorability.

5.1.4 Online Presence

Website and Social Media: Create a professional website that serves as the central hub of your online presence. Additionally, be active on relevant social networks for your industry. Share valuable content, connect with other professionals, and engage in discussions to increase your visibility.

5.1.5 Quality Content

Demonstration of Knowledge: Produce and share relevant and valuable content. This may include blogs, articles, videos, or podcasts that demonstrate your expertise in the field. Quality content helps build authority and attracts the attention of potential clients and partners.

5.1.6 Testimonials and Recommendations

Social Validation: Request and display testimonials and recommendations from satisfied clients. These social validations are crucial for building the trust of future clients, highlighting your skills, and the quality of your work.

5.1.7 Networking

Professional Relationships: Attend industry events, conferences, and networking gatherings. Establish genuine connections with other professionals, potential clients, and industry influencers. Networking is a powerful tool in personal brand building.

5.1.8 Continuous Development

Constant Professional Improvement: Demonstrate your commitment to continuous improvement. Stay updated with the latest industry trends, participate in relevant courses and workshops, and share your professional achievements on your platform.

By building your initial personal brand with authenticity and strategy, you create a solid foundation to attract the attention and trust of your target audience. In the next topic, we will explore more specific marketing strategies to effectively promote your services.

Marketing Strategies

5.2 Effective Marketing Strategies

In addition to building your personal brand, it's essential to implement effective marketing strategies to promote your services and reach your target audience. In this topic, we will explore some practical strategies to increase the visibility of your service-based business.

5.2.1 Content Marketing

Regular and Relevant Production: Content marketing remains one of the most powerful strategies. Regularly produce relevant content for your audience, such as blogs, videos, infographics, or webinars. This not only demonstrates your expertise but also attracts and retains the attention of your audience.

5.2.2 SEO (Search Engine Optimization)

Online Visibility: Optimize your website and content for search engines. Use relevant keywords for your industry and create a solid SEO strategy to increase your online visibility, making it easier for potential clients to find you.

5.2.3 Social Media Marketing

Engagement and Sharing: Utilize social media platforms strategically. Engage in relevant conversations, share your content, interact with your audience, and use targeted ads. Social media marketing is a powerful tool for building relationships and increasing exposure.

5.2.4 Email Marketing

Direct and Personalized Communication: Build an email list and implement email marketing strategies. Send newsletters, service updates, and exclusive content directly to your audience's inbox. Email marketing allows for more direct and personalized communication.

5.2.5 Strategic Partnerships

Mutually Beneficial Collaborations: Establish strategic partnerships with other professionals or related companies. This may include co-organizing events, sharing content, or referral programs. Partnerships can expand your reach and attract new business opportunities.

5.2.6 Events and Webinars

Presence and Education: Participate in industry events, conferences, or host webinars. These activities not only increase your market presence but also provide opportunities to educate your audience about your services and skills.

5.2.7 Promotions and Strategic Discounts

Attractions for New Clients: Consider strategic promotions or discounts to attract new clients. This can be particularly effective in the early stages of your business, encouraging trial and building loyalty.

5.2.8 Monitoring and Results Analysis

Constant Adaptation: Implement analytics tools to monitor the performance of your marketing strategies. Be prepared to adapt your approaches based on data and metrics, continually optimizing your campaigns.

By incorporating these effective marketing strategies, you create an environment conducive to the growth of your service-based business.

Utilization of Social Media

5.3 Utilization of Social Media

Social media plays a crucial role in personal marketing and effective promotion of services provided. In this topic, we will explore specific strategies for using social media efficiently, maximizing reach and interaction with your target audience.

5.3.1 Strategic Platform Selection

Identification of Target Audience: Select social media platforms based on your target audience. Understand where your audience is most active and tailor your strategies for those platforms. For example, LinkedIn may be more effective for professional services, while Instagram may be ideal for visual content.

5.3.2 Creation of Professional Profile

Coherent and Professional Presentation: Optimize your social media profiles to reflect a professional image. This includes using a professional profile picture, a concise biography, and relevant information about your services. Ensure visual and message consistency across all platforms.

5.3.3 Relevant and Engaging Content

Sharing Value: Produce and share content relevant to your target audience. This may include tips, industry insights, success stories, or even behind-the-scenes of your work. Engaging content creates deeper connections and demonstrates your expertise in the field.

5.3.4 Frequency and Consistency

Maintaining Online Presence: Maintain a consistent online presence. Post regularly, engage with comments and messages, and stay updated on the latest trends and news relevant to your field. Consistency helps build and maintain your audience's interest.

5.3.5 Use of Visual Media

Visual Attraction: Leverage visual media, such as images and videos, to increase the attractiveness of your posts. Visual materials are more likely to be shared and retained by users, expanding the reach of your messages.

5.3.6 Participation in Groups and Communities

Engagement Beyond Personal Profile: Actively participate in relevant groups and communities. In addition to promoting your services on your personal profile, participation in groups provides an opportunity to build relationships, share knowledge, and expand your network.

5.3.7 Targeted Advertising

Specific Targeting: Consider using targeted ads to expand the reach of your messages. Social media platforms offer powerful targeting tools, allowing you to reach a specific audience more accurately.

5.3.8 Metrics Analysis and Feedback

Continuous Improvement: Regularly analyze performance metrics on social media. Understand what is working, which types of content generate more interactions, and adapt your strategies based on feedback and analysis.

By using social media strategically, you can create a robust online presence, build meaningful relationships, and effectively promote your services. In the next chapter, we will explore essential customer service practices to ensure customer satisfaction and loyalty.

Chapter 6

Customer Management

6.1 Establishing a Professional Relationship

The foundation of a successful service-based business lies in the ability to build and maintain strong professional relationships with clients. In this first topic, we will explore strategies for establishing a professional relationship from the outset, promoting trust and customer satisfaction.

6.1.1 Deep Understanding of Customer Needs

Initial Interviews and Diagnostics: Before embarking on any project, conduct detailed interviews and diagnostics to understand the specific needs of the customer. Demonstrating a genuine interest in understanding the client's goals and challenges establishes a solid foundation for collaboration.

6.1.2 Transparency about Processes and Expectations

Clear Communication from the Start: Establish clear communication about processes, timelines, and expectations from the outset of the relationship. This prevents future misunderstandings and provides the client with a transparent view of what to expect when working with you.

6.1.3 Detailed Contracts and Written Agreements

Formal Documentation: Draft detailed contracts that address all aspects of the service to be provided. This includes project scope, deadlines, fees, payment terms, and any other relevant information. Having agreements in writing helps to avoid conflicts and provides security for both parties.

6.1.4 Goal Setting and Performance Indicators

Establishment of Measurable Milestones: Along with the client, set clear goals and performance indicators that can be measured throughout the project. This not only aligns expectations but also provides a framework for evaluating success and making adjustments as necessary.

6.1.5 Proactive Communication

Regular Updates and Feedback: Maintain proactive communication with the client. Provide regular updates on project progress, discuss any challenges that may arise, and be open to client feedback. Constant communication builds trust and reassures the client about the progress of the work.

6.1.6 Personalization of Service

Understanding Individual Preferences: Tailor your service to each client's individual preferences. Some clients may prefer more frequent communication, while others may value more consolidated updates. Understand preferences to offer a more personalized service.

6.1.7 Proactive Problem Resolution

Anticipation and Swift Resolution: Anticipate potential problems and be prepared to resolve challenges quickly. A proactive approach to problem-solving demonstrates commitment and strengthens the client's trust in your ability to manage adverse situations.

6.1.8 Post-Service and Post-Project Feedback

Evaluation and Continuous Improvement: After completing the service, request feedback from the client. Analyze the positives and areas for improvement. Additionally, be open to discussions about future projects and how the partnership can evolve.

By establishing a strong professional relationship from the outset, you lay the groundwork for a successful collaboration and lasting customer satisfaction.

Communication

6.2 Effective Communication

Communication is the backbone of successful customer management. In this topic, we will explore strategies to ensure effective communication throughout the entire service delivery cycle, promoting mutual understanding and strengthening the client relationship.

6.2.1 Active Listening

Deep Understanding of Needs: Practice active listening in all interactions with the client. Be fully present, ask clarifying questions, and demonstrate genuine interest in the client's concerns and expectations. Active listening builds a solid foundation for effective communication.

6.2.2 Clear and Concise Communication

Avoid Ambiguity and Misunderstandings: Prioritize clarity and conciseness in all communications. Avoid complex jargon and provide information straightforwardly. This reduces the likelihood of misunderstandings and ensures that all parties are aligned.

6.2.3 Use of Various Communication Channels

Adaptation to Client's Preferred Style: Acknowledge that each client may have different communication preferences. Some may prefer detailed emails, while others may find a phone call or in-person meeting more effective. Adapt to the client's preferred styles to optimize communication.

6.2.4 Schedule Regular Meetings

Maintaining Open Lines of Communication: Establish a schedule of regular meetings with the client. This provides a dedicated forum for discussions, updates, and problem resolution. Consistent meetings keep lines of communication open and demonstrate commitment to the project's success.

6.2.5 Transparent Status Updates

Transparency about Progress: Provide transparent status updates on the project's progress. This not only informs the client about achievements but also allows proactive adjustments if challenges or scope changes arise.

6.2.6 Prompt Response to Client Communications

Agility in Response: Demonstrate agility in responding to client communications. Quick responses convey professionalism and show that the client is a priority. Even if you don't have a definitive answer, inform the client that you are working on the issue.

6.2.7 Clear Performance Reports

Transparency about Results: Present clear and understandable performance reports. Highlight key milestones achieved, key metrics, and areas for improvement. Performance reports provide an objective view of the value delivered to the client.

6.2.8 Respect for Feedback Channels

Welcoming Opinions and Suggestions: Actively encourage client feedback and demonstrate respect for their opinions and suggestions. Use feedback to adjust your practices and continuously improve the quality of service offered.

By adopting effective communication strategies, you promote mutual understanding and also strengthen client trust and satisfaction. In the next topic, we will explore strategies for handling challenging situations and resolving conflicts constructively in customer management.

Conflict Resolution

6.3 Conflict Resolution

Customer management may involve challenges and conflicts that require a careful approach to preserve the relationship and achieve constructive solutions. In this topic, we will explore effective strategies for dealing with conflicts proactively, promoting resolution, and strengthening the partnership.

6.3.1 Proactive Approach

Early Identification of Conflict Signs: Develop the ability to identify early signs of conflict. Be alert to changes in communication tone, unexpected delays, or any signs of client dissatisfaction. Addressing problems before they escalate into crises is crucial.

6.3.2 Empathetic Listening

Deep Understanding of Concerns: When a conflict arises, practice empathetic listening. Allow the client to share their concerns and feelings, demonstrating understanding and empathy. This creates an environment conducive to constructive resolution.

6.3.3 Transparent Communication

Clarity in Presenting Points of View: Communicate your point of view and intentions clearly and transparently. Open communication helps dispel misunderstandings and establishes a basis for conflict resolution.

6.3.4 Identification of Common Interests

Focus on Solutions Beneficial to Both Parties: When exploring solutions, identify common interests. Seek alternatives that benefit both parties, demonstrating a collaborative approach to conflict resolution.

6.3.5 Development of Creative Solutions

Thinking "Outside the Box": Be open to creative solutions that can resolve the conflict innovatively. Sometimes, an unconventional approach can lead to outcomes that benefit both parties.

6.3.6 External Mediation

Involvement of Impartial Third Parties: If the conflict persists, consider involving an external mediator. This could be a conflict resolution specialist who acts impartially, facilitating communication and seeking equitable solutions.

6.3.7 Commitment to Continuous Improvement

Learning from Conflicts: View conflicts as learning opportunities. Evaluate each conflict situation to identify areas for improvement in processes, communication, or internal procedures.

6.3.8 Proper Documentation

Recording Agreements and Solutions: After resolving the conflict, properly document the agreements reached. This provides a clear reference for both parties and helps prevent future misunderstandings.

6.3.9 Post-Conflict Evaluation

Verification of Solution Effectiveness: Conduct post-conflict evaluations to ensure that the implemented solutions are effective. If necessary, make adjustments to continuously improve processes and prevent recurrences.

By adopting effective conflict resolution strategies, you turn potential challenges into opportunities to strengthen the client relationship. In the next chapter, we will explore strategies to continuously enhance your services, ensuring excellence in customer service delivery.

Chapter 7

Service Delivery

7.1 Best Practices

Effective service delivery is not only about delivering the final product but also about the overall customer experience. In this first topic, we will explore essential best practices that contribute to exceptional service delivery, strengthening customer satisfaction and your business's reputation.

7.1.1 Deep Understanding of Needs

Detailed Diagnosis: Before starting any project or service, take time to deeply understand the customer's needs and expectations. Conduct detailed interviews, ask clarifying questions, and ensure that all parties have a clear understanding of the scope of work.

7.1.2 Transparent Communication

Regular Updates and Clarifications: Maintain transparent communication throughout the project. Provide regular updates on progress, promptly clarify doubts, and be open to discussions. Transparency builds trust and reassures the customer about the progress of the service.

7.1.3 Deadline Compliance

Effective Time Management: Meeting deadlines is crucial for customer satisfaction. Adopt effective time management practices, set realistic deadlines, and proactively communicate any delays, providing explanations and solutions if necessary.

7.1.4 Service Personalization

Adaptation to Individual Preferences: Recognize that each customer is unique. Tailor the service according to individual preferences, considering communication styles, expectations, and specific needs of each customer. Personalization demonstrates genuine commitment to customer satisfaction.

7.1.5 Proactive Problem Solving

Anticipation and Swift Resolution: Anticipate potential problems and be prepared to resolve them quickly. A proactive approach to problem-solving demonstrates commitment and reinforces the customer's confidence in your ability to manage challenges.

7.1.6 Consistent Quality

High Standards at Every Stage: Maintain high-quality standards at every stage of the service. From planning to final delivery, ensure that every aspect of the service meets or exceeds customer expectations. Consistency in quality builds a solid reputation.

7.1.7 Exceptional Customer Service

Courtesy and Professionalism: Provide exceptional customer service in every interaction. Be courteous, professional, and ready to address questions or concerns effectively. Customer service is an extension of your service and can significantly influence the customer experience.

7.1.8 Continuous Feedback

Requesting and Applying Feedback: Regularly solicit feedback from the customer and use this information to continuously improve your services. Being open to feedback demonstrates a commitment to continuous improvement and allows for adjustments as per customer needs.

7.1.9 Value Addition

Beyond Expectations: Look for opportunities to add value to the service. This may include offering additional information, complementary resources, or innovative solutions that exceed customer expectations. Value addition strengthens the customer's positive perception of the service received.

Incorporating these best practices in service delivery satisfies customer needs and also builds lasting relationships and establishes a positive reputation in the market.

Project Management

7.2 Project Management

Project management is a fundamental piece in effective service delivery. In this topic, we will explore strategies and essential best practices to ensure efficient project management, from planning to delivery, contributing to the success of the service provided.

7.2.1 Detailed Planning

Clear Project Structure: Before starting any project, dedicate time to detailed planning. Clearly define the objectives, scope, necessary resources, deadlines, and project stages. Structured planning serves as the foundation for efficient execution.

7.2.2 Competent and Motivated Team

Careful Selection of Collaborators: Assemble a competent and motivated team for the project. Assess the necessary skills and assign tasks according to individual competencies. Keep the team informed about the project's objectives and impact to maintain motivation.

7.2.3 Clear Definition of Responsibilities

Precise Assignments: Each team member should have defined responsibilities and understand their role in the project. Clarity in assignments prevents confusion, improves efficiency, and allows for more precise progress monitoring.

7.2.4 Efficient Communication

Clear Channels and Adequate Frequency: Establish efficient communication channels and determine the frequency of updates. Clear communication within the team and with the client is essential to keep everyone informed about the project status and any changes.

7.2.5 Continuous Progress Monitoring

Regular Assessment of Milestones: Continuously monitor the project's progress against established milestones. If there are deviations, adjust the plan as necessary. Regular monitoring helps anticipate potential issues and keep the project on track.

7.2.6 Adaptation to Changes

Flexibility and Resilience: Be prepared to deal with changes in project scope, deadlines, or requirements. Flexibility and resilience are essential to adapt to evolving demands and maintain delivery within expectations.

7.2.7 Risk Management

Early Identification and Mitigation: Proactively identify potential project risks and develop mitigation plans. Risk management helps anticipate challenges and implement preventive measures to avoid negative impacts.

7.2.8 Post-Project Evaluation

Analysis of Lessons Learned: After completing the project, conduct a post-project evaluation. Identify what worked well, areas for improvement, and lessons learned. Use this information to enhance your processes and approaches in future projects.

7.2.9 Delivery and Results Evaluation

Effective Conclusion and Results Evaluation: At the end of the project, ensure delivery of results as agreed upon. Additionally, evaluate with the client satisfaction with the service provided. Post-delivery evaluation is valuable to understand customer perceptions and identify opportunities for improvement.

Incorporating effective project management practices ensures successful service delivery, meeting customer expectations, and maintaining a high standard of quality. In the next topic, we will explore strategies to cultivate customer loyalty and promote continuous customer return to your business.

Quality Customer Service

7.3 Quality Customer Service

Quality customer service plays a crucial role in building strong relationships with clients. In this topic, we will explore strategies and essential best practices to ensure high-quality service, promoting customer satisfaction, and strengthening your business's reputation.

7.3.1 Empathy and Understanding

Putting Yourself in the Customer's Shoes: Demonstrating empathy is fundamental to providing quality service. Put yourself in the customer's shoes, understand their needs and concerns, and show genuine interest in solving their problems.

7.3.2 Speed and Efficiency

Quick Responses and Efficient Solutions: Prioritize quick responses and efficiency in problem resolution. Customers value agility in service, and resolving issues effectively contributes to a positive experience.

7.3.3 Clear and Respectful Communication

Expressing Ideas Clearly: Maintain clear and respectful communication in all interactions. Avoid complicated jargon, explain information in an understandable manner, and treat the customer with courtesy. Transparent communication builds trust.

7.3.4 Personalization of Service

Adaptation to Individual Preferences: Recognize the individual preferences of each customer. Some may prefer email communication, while others may prefer a phone call. Personalize the service according to the customer's needs and preferences.

7.3.5 Continuous Team Training

Skills and Knowledge Updates: Keep your team continuously trained and updated in customer service skills. This includes developing communication skills, problem-solving abilities, and a deep understanding of the services offered.

7.3.6 Positive and Constructive Feedback

Recognition and Improvement Opportunities: Provide regular feedback to the team, recognizing positive practices and offering constructive guidance for improvement. Feedback is a valuable tool to motivate the team and enhance service quality.

7.3.7 Post-Sale Treatment

Post-Service Follow-Up: After the service is completed, conduct post-sale follow-ups to ensure ongoing customer satisfaction. Be available to address additional questions and show that the relationship goes beyond project completion.

7.3.8 Proactive Problem Resolution

Anticipation and Quick Resolution: Anticipate potential problems and be prepared to resolve them promptly. A proactive approach to problem-solving demonstrates commitment and reinforces the customer's confidence in your ability to manage challenges.

7.3.9 Continuous Customer Satisfaction Assessment

Feedback Solicitation and Analysis: Regularly solicit feedback from customers about the service received. Analyze this information to identify areas for improvement and adjust strategies as necessary.

By adopting effective practices for quality customer service, you not only meet customer expectations but also build a solid reputation and foster customer loyalty.

Chapter 8

Legal and Contractual Aspects

8.1 Contract Drafting

Drafting contracts is a crucial part of service provision, ensuring clarity and security for both parties involved. In this first topic, we will explore best practices in contract drafting to protect your interests, establish clear expectations, and promote healthy business relationships.

8.1.1 Precise Definition of Services

Detailed Scope of Work: Start the contract by precisely and comprehensively defining the services to be provided. Specify the scope of work, goals to be achieved, and any specific deliverables expected. This provides a clear understanding of what is included in the service.

8.1.2 Payment Terms and Fees

Transparent Financial Terms: Clearly establish payment terms, including deadlines and acceptable payment methods. Additionally, specify the fees for the services rendered. Transparency in these areas prevents misunderstandings and establishes clear financial expectations.

8.1.3 Deadlines and Schedule

Setting Time Limits: Include deadlines and a schedule in the contract for each phase of the project. This not only guides the client on time expectations but also provides a means to assess service performance over time.

8.1.4 Responsibilities and Duties

Clear Assignments for Both Parties: Detail the responsibilities and duties of both parties involved in the contract. This includes not only the service provider's obligations but also the client's responsibilities, ensuring effective collaboration.

8.1.5 Termination Clauses

Procedures in Case of Cancellation: Include termination clauses that define procedures in case of contract cancellation by both parties. This helps protect the interests of both parties in unforeseen situations.

8.1.6 Intellectual Property

Agreement on Ownership of Work: Clearly specify intellectual property issues in the contract. If there is the creation of intellectual property during the service provision, determine who holds the rights and how they can be utilized.

8.1.7 Confidentiality Clauses

Protection of Sensitive Information: Include confidentiality clauses to protect sensitive information shared during service provision. These clauses help ensure the security and privacy of business information.

8.1.8 Dispute Resolution Mechanisms

Procedures in Case of Conflicts: Anticipate potential conflicts by including dispute resolution mechanisms in the contract. This may include mediation or arbitration, offering a faster and more efficient approach than judicial litigation.

8.1.9 Legal Review

Consultation with Legal Professionals: Before signing the contract, it is recommended to have it legally reviewed by specialized professionals. This ensures that the contract complies with applicable laws and protects both parties from potential legal complications.

8.1.10 Contractual Updates

Flexibility for Changes: Include clauses that allow contractual updates when necessary. This provides flexibility to adjust the contract in case of changes in circumstances or the scope of service.

By following these practices in contract drafting, you establish a solid foundation for legally secure and transparent service provision. In the next topic, we will explore other legal and regulatory considerations that may impact service provision.

Rights and Duties

8.2 Rights and Duties of the Service Provider

The clear establishment of the rights and duties of the service provider is essential to ensure transparency, legal compliance, and healthy business relationships. In this topic, we will explore the key elements to consider when defining the rights and duties of the service provider in contracts.

8.2.1 Compliance with Agreed Scope

Delivery as Established: It is a fundamental duty of the service provider to comply with the agreed scope in the contract. This includes delivering services according to the specified requirements, deadlines, and quality agreed upon, ensuring that the client receives what was contracted.

8.2.2 Professional Competence

Maintenance of Competence Standards: The service provider has the right and duty to perform the contracted tasks with professional competence. This involves staying updated with industry best practices, utilizing specialized skills and knowledge, and striving for excellence in delivery.

8.2.3 Protection of Intellectual Property

Respect for Intellectual Property Rights: The service provider must respect intellectual property rights, ensuring that there is no infringement of patents, copyrights, or other intellectual properties. If the contract involves the creation of new materials, it is essential to clearly establish who holds the rights.

8.2.4 Maintenance of Confidentiality

Preservation of Sensitive Information: The service provider generally assumes the duty to maintain the confidentiality of the client's sensitive information. This commitment aims to protect business data, strategies, and other confidential elements that may be shared during the provision of services.

8.2.5 Transparent Communication

Duty to Communicate Transparently: The service provider has the duty to maintain transparent communication with the client. This includes reporting progress on work, informing about encountered challenges, and providing regular updates to ensure that the client is well-informed about the service status.

8.2.6 Problem Resolution

Proactive Approach to Problem Solving: Faced with challenges or issues during the provision of services, the provider has the duty to address them proactively. This includes the early identification of potential obstacles, transparent communication about these challenges, and seeking effective solutions in collaboration with the client.

8.2.7 Right to Remuneration

Compensation for Services Rendered: The service provider has the right to remuneration for the services rendered, as agreed upon in the contract. This right includes receiving fees, agreed-upon expenses, and any other form of compensation stipulated in the contract.

8.2.8 Compliance with Laws and Regulations

Compliance with Relevant Legislation: The service provider has the duty to comply with all laws and regulations relevant to their area of operation. This includes tax matters, industry-specific regulations, and other legal requirements applicable to the service provided.

8.2.9 Contract Termination

Right and Duty of Termination: Both parties, including the service provider, have the right to terminate the contract under certain conditions. This right must be exercised in accordance with the termination clauses agreed upon in the contract, including notification and proper procedures.

Dispute Resolution

8.3 Dispute Resolution

The possibility of disputes is a reality in business, but appropriate resolution strategies can minimize negative impacts and preserve relationships. In this topic, we will explore best practices for effectively resolving disputes, ensuring that conflicts are addressed fairly and efficiently.

8.3.1 Dispute Resolution Clauses

Inclusion of Alternative Mechanisms: In the contract, include clauses establishing alternative dispute resolution mechanisms, such as mediation or arbitration. These methods offer a faster and less adversarial approach than traditional judicial litigation.

8.3.2 Good-Faith Negotiation

Seeking Mutually Acceptable Solutions: When a conflict arises, promote good-faith negotiation between the parties. Encourage the search for mutually acceptable solutions, prioritizing dialogue and collaboration over an adversarial approach.

8.3.3 Mediation

Involvement of Impartial Third Parties: Mediation involves the presence of an impartial third party who facilitates communication between the parties and helps in reaching an agreement. Consider mediation as an option before resorting to more formal legal processes.

8.3.4 Arbitration

Decision by an Independent Arbitrator: Arbitration involves an independent arbitrator who makes a binding decision on the dispute. This is an alternative to judicial litigation and can offer a quicker and more efficient solution.

8.3.5 Judicial Litigation

Last Resort: Judicial litigation is the last resort and is often more time-consuming and costly. However, in some cases, it may be the only option. Ensure that contract clauses regarding judicial litigation are clear and detailed.

8.3.6 Risk and Cost Assessment

Pre-Decision Risk and Cost Analysis: Before choosing a dispute resolution method, carefully assess the risks and costs associated with each option. Consider factors such as time, legal expenses, and the potential impact on business relationships.

8.3.7 Compliance with Contractual Clauses

Ensuring Adherence to Contractual Provisions: Both parties must comply with contractual clauses related to dispute resolution. This includes following the procedures established in the contract to resolve disputes, ensuring that both parties are treated fairly.

8.3.8 Specialized Legal Professionals

Consultation with Specialized Lawyers: In litigation situations, seeking guidance from lawyers specialized in dispute resolution or the specific area of the contract can be crucial. Specialized legal professionals can offer valuable insights and effective representation.

8.3.9 Adequate Documentation

Detailed Recording of Events: Maintain detailed documentation of all events related to the dispute. This may include communications, contracts, meeting records, and any relevant correspondence. Adequate documentation strengthens the position of both parties in any chosen resolution method.

8.3.10 Relationship Preservation

Prioritizing the Business Relationship: Even amidst litigation, seek to preserve the business relationship whenever possible. Dispute resolution should not only be about winning or losing but also about maintaining professional relationships that may be valuable in the future.

By adopting effective dispute resolution strategies, you will mitigate the negative impact of these situations and maintain the integrity of your business.

Chapter 9

Useful Tools and Resources

9.1 Software and Applications for Management

Efficient management is essential for success in service delivery. In this first topic, we will explore various tools and applications that can optimize your business management, providing greater operational efficiency, organization, and better control over activities.

9.1.1 Enterprise Resource Planning (ERP) Systems:

ERPs integrate various areas of the business, such as finance, human resources, sales, and logistics. Tools like SAP, Oracle NetSuite, and Microsoft Dynamics offer comprehensive solutions for more integrated and efficient management.

9.1.2 Project Management Tools:

For effective project management, applications like Asana, Trello, and Microsoft Project are invaluable. These tools facilitate task tracking, document sharing, and communication between teams.

9.1.3 Communication and Collaboration Platforms:

Success in service delivery often depends on efficient communication. Tools like Slack,

Microsoft Teams, and Zoom offer collaborative virtual environments, facilitating communication within the team and with clients.

9.1.4 Accounting Tools:

Financial management is crucial. Tools like QuickBooks, Xero, and Sage facilitate accounting, billing, and financial control, ensuring a clear view of the business's financial health.

9.1.5 Customer Relationship Management (CRM):

To strengthen customer relationships, CRMs like Salesforce, HubSpot, and Zoho CRM are essential. These platforms help manage contacts, record interactions, and personalize service strategies.

9.1.6 Marketing Automation Tools:

Automating marketing processes can save time and improve effectiveness. Tools like HubSpot, Mailchimp, and Marketo assist in email automation, campaigns, and result analysis.

9.1.7 Task Management Software:

Keeping tasks organized is vital. Tools like Todoist, Wunderlist (or its successor Microsoft To Do), and Remember The Milk aid in daily organization and activity tracking.

9.1.8 Cloud Storage Platforms:

To facilitate document access and sharing, cloud storage is essential. Services like Google Drive,

Dropbox, and Microsoft OneDrive offer secure and collaborative solutions.

9.1.9 Video Conferencing and Webinar Software:

With the growing need for virtual communication, tools like Zoom, Microsoft Teams, and Webex are essential for online meetings, presentations, and training.

9.1.10 Cybersecurity Tools:

Protecting sensitive data is a priority. Tools like Norton, McAfee, and Bitdefender offer cybersecurity solutions, protecting against online threats.

9.1.11 Data Analytics Platforms:

To make informed decisions, data analytics tools like Tableau, Google Analytics, and Microsoft Power BI offer valuable insights into business performance.

By incorporating these tools into your practice, you will strengthen your business management, ensuring greater efficiency and alignment with the demands of service delivery. In the next topic, we will explore ethical considerations in service delivery and how these principles can positively impact your professional practice.

Marketing Platforms

9.2 Online Marketing Platforms

In a highly competitive digital landscape, online marketing platforms play a crucial role in promoting and increasing the visibility of services provided. In this topic, we will explore some of the key online marketing platforms that can boost your business's presence on the internet.

9.2.1 Google Ads:

Google Ads is a powerful advertising platform that allows you to create ads that appear in Google search results, on partner websites, and on YouTube. With precise targeting, you can direct your ads to the right audience.

9.2.2 Facebook Ads:

With a huge user base, Facebook Ads offers a robust platform for creating targeted ads. You can target your audience based on demographics, interests, and behaviors, increasing the effectiveness of your campaign.

9.2.3 Instagram for Business:

Instagram is a powerful visual platform, especially for businesses focused on visual content. Instagram for Business offers analytics and promotion tools to boost brand visibility through captivating photos and videos.

9.2.4 LinkedIn Advertising:

If your business focuses on B2B services, LinkedIn Advertising is essential. It allows you to target ads based on job titles, industries, and companies, reaching relevant professionals in your field.

9.2.5 Twitter for Business:

Twitter for Business offers promotion opportunities through sponsored tweets and ads. It's an effective platform for increasing brand visibility and engaging with your target audience through short and direct messages.

9.2.6 YouTube Advertising:

YouTube is the world's largest video-sharing platform. Ads on YouTube can reach a vast audience, and you can target your ads based on interests, keywords, and viewing behaviors.

9.2.7 Email Marketing Platforms:

Tools like Mailchimp, Sendinblue, and Constant Contact are essential for email marketing strategies. They allow you to create customized campaigns, automate workflows, and track important metrics.

9.2.8 SEO Tools:

Search Engine Optimization (SEO) is crucial for online visibility. Tools like SEMrush, Moz, and Ahrefs help optimize your website, conduct competitor analysis, and improve your ranking in search results.

9.2.9 Content Marketing Platforms:

Platforms like HubSpot, CoSchedule, and ContentStudio are ideal for managing content marketing strategies. They offer features for content creation, scheduling, and analysis, contributing to organic growth.

9.2.10 Google Analytics:

To understand online performance, Google Analytics is essential. It provides detailed insights into website traffic, user behavior, and campaign effectiveness, allowing for strategic adjustments.

9.2.11 Live Video Channels:

Platforms like Facebook Live, Instagram Live, and YouTube Live offer opportunities to connect in real-time with your audience. Live video is a valuable tool for engagement and direct interaction.

By strategically incorporating these online marketing platforms into your approach, you will increase your business's visibility, effectively reaching your target audience.

Networking

9.3 Networking Resources

Networking is a fundamental part of building and growing a service-based business. In this topic, we will explore various tools and resources that can boost your networking initiatives, connecting you with professionals, clients, and business opportunities.

9.3.1 LinkedIn:

LinkedIn is a widely used professional networking platform. In addition to creating a robust professional profile, you can join relevant groups in your field, share insights, and connect with professionals who can be valuable for your business.

9.3.2 Online Events and Conferences:

Participating in online events and conferences provides valuable networking opportunities. Platforms like Eventbrite, Meetup, and Zoom make it easy to attend events related to your industry, enabling meaningful connections.

9.3.3 Local Networking Tools:

To build connections in your local community, utilize tools like Nextdoor, local Facebook groups, and region-specific apps. This facilitates connecting with other local service providers and potential clients.

9.3.4 Networking CRM:

Maintaining a networking CRM is an effective practice. Tools like Contactually and Nimble help manage your contacts, follow-up reminders, and past interactions, strengthening your relationships over time.

9.3.5 Alumni Networks:

If you attended an educational institution, leverage alumni networks. Platforms like Graduway and AlumniFinder allow you to connect with fellow alumni, creating valuable networking opportunities.

9.3.6 Professional Collaboration Platforms:

Tools like Slack, Microsoft Teams, and Trello are not just for internal collaboration. They can also be used to connect with other professionals in your industry, participate in communities, and exchange knowledge.

9.3.7 Clubs and Professional Associations:

Joining relevant clubs and professional associations in your field is an effective networking strategy. Participation in meetings and events of these organizations can open doors to new opportunities.

9.3.8 Question and Answer Platforms:

Participating in platforms like Quora and Reddit allows you to not only share your knowledge but also connect with professionals and potential clients seeking guidance in your area of expertise.

9.3.9 Professional Networking Apps:

Some apps are specifically designed to facilitate professional networking. Examples include Shapr, Bumble Bizz, and Weave, which connect professionals with similar interests.

9.3.10 Online Webinars and Workshops:

Hosting online webinars and workshops not only showcases your expertise but also creates networking opportunities. Platforms like Zoom and Webex allow real-time interactions and can attract a diverse audience.

9.3.11 Freelancer Platforms:

If you are an independent service provider, platforms like Upwork, Freelancer, and Fiverr not only offer job opportunities but also enable you to build a network of clients and colleagues.

By leveraging these networking tools, you will build a strong professional network, opening doors for collaborations, partnerships, and growth opportunities for your business.

Chapter 10

Continuous Professional Development

10.1 Participation in Events and Workshops

Continuous professional development is essential to stay relevant in an ever-evolving business landscape. Participating in events and workshops is a valuable strategy to acquire new knowledge, develop skills, and expand your network of contacts. In this first topic, we will explore the importance and best practices to make the most of these learning opportunities.

10.1.1 Importance of Participation in Events:

- **Knowledge Update:** Attending events provides access to recent information and trends in your field. Lectures, panels, and presentations offer valuable insights that can drive innovation in your services.

- **Professional Networking:** Events are conducive environments to build and strengthen your professional network. Connecting with industry colleagues, experts, and potential clients can result in strategic partnerships and business opportunities.

- **Inspiration and Motivation:** Contact with inspiring professionals and success stories can motivate and energize your own work.

Sharing experiences and challenges at events provides a unique perspective that can drive your professional growth.

10.1.2 Strategic Event Selection:

- **Alignment with Professional Goals:** Select events that align with your professional goals. Consider areas where you want to enhance your skills, explore new trends, or expand your network of contacts.

- **Diversity of Formats:** Choose events that offer a variety of formats, such as lectures, interactive workshops, practical sessions, and networking opportunities. This will provide a more comprehensive experience.

10.1.3 Preparation and Effective Engagement:

- **Pre-Event Program Study:** Before the event, study the program to identify sessions and speakers of interest. This allows you to maximize your time and participate in activities most relevant to your goals.

- **Active Participation in Discussions:** Contribute to discussions and ask questions during sessions. This not only demonstrates your engagement but also provides opportunities to interact with speakers and other participants.

10.1.4 Strategic Networking:

- **Business Cards and Online Profile:** Have updated business cards and create an online profile that highlights your skills and experiences. This facilitates the exchange of information during events and helps contacts remember you afterward.

- **Participation in Networking Activities:** Take advantage of networking activities offered by events, such as cocktails, coffee breaks, and roundtable discussions. These informal moments are ideal for establishing more personal connections.

10.1.5 Post-Event Utilization:

- **Follow-Up with Contacts:** After the event, follow up with the contacts you made. Send personalized emails, connect on social networks, and explore collaboration opportunities that may arise from these connections.

- **Practical Application of Knowledge:** Implement the knowledge gained in your daily work. Practical application is essential to transform information into effective actions and improve your professional performance.

By actively participating in events and workshops, you invest not only in developing your skills but also in building a solid and valuable network.

Continuing Education

10.2 Continuing Education

Continuing education is an essential pillar for professionals seeking to stay updated and competitive in their fields of expertise. In this second topic, we will explore the importance of continuing education, its various forms, and effective strategies to ensure continuous learning throughout one's career.

10.2.1 Importance of Continuing Education:

- **Knowledge Update:** The rapid evolution of industries demands that professionals stay constantly updated. Continuing education is key to understanding new technologies, market trends, and innovations in the field.

- **Maintenance of Professional Relevance:** Professionals who constantly seek to improve their skills and knowledge remain relevant in a dynamic job market. This not only preserves employability but also contributes to career advancement opportunities.

10.2.2 Forms of Continuing Education:

- **In-Person and Online Courses:** The offering of in-person and online courses is vast. Platforms like Coursera, Udemy, and LinkedIn Learning provide access to a variety of courses in diverse areas, allowing flexibility to learn at one's own pace.

- **Professional Certifications:** Certifications are recognized as tangible evidence of knowledge and skills. Seeking relevant certifications for your field of expertise is an effective way to validate your competencies with employers and clients.

- **Participation in Lectures and Seminars:** Lectures and seminars offer the opportunity to learn from experts, discuss relevant topics, and broaden understanding of challenges and trends in the industry.

10.2.3 Efficient Strategies for Continuing Education:

- **Establishment of Clear Goals:** Define clear educational goals, identifying specific areas you wish to improve. These goals will serve as guidelines for selecting courses and learning activities.

- **Regular Study Schedule:** Set aside time regularly for studying and learning. Creating a dedicated schedule for continuing education ensures consistency and prevents this practice from being neglected in your professional routine.

- **Participation in Professional Communities:** Engage in online and offline professional communities. Exchanging knowledge and experiences with colleagues broadens your perspective and provides continuous learning through collaborative interactions.

10.2.4 Investment in Personal Development:

- **Development of Complementary Skills:** In addition to technical skills, invest in complementary skills such as leadership, communication, and problem-solving. These competencies are increasingly valued in the workplace.

- **Exploration of New Areas:** Be open to exploring new areas related to your profession. This expands your skill set and allows you to excel in multifaceted aspects of your field.

10.2.5 Feedback and Continuous Evaluation:

- **Seeking Feedback:** Regularly seek feedback from colleagues, mentors, or instructors. Constructive feedback helps identify areas for improvement and adapt your learning approach.

- **Continuous Progress Evaluation:** Regularly assess your progress in relation to established goals. This allows you to adjust your continuing education plan as needed and stay aligned with your objectives.

10.2.6 Mentoring and Counseling:

- **Seeking Mentors:** Establish relationships with experienced professionals who can guide you in your professional development. Mentoring is a valuable tool for gaining insights, practical advice, and guidance in continuing education.

By incorporating continuing education as a constant practice in your career, you will be equipped to tackle the dynamic challenges of the market and thrive in constantly evolving professional environments.

Adaptation to Changes

10.3 Adaptation to Market Changes

The ability to adapt is a crucial skill for professionals seeking to stand out in a constantly evolving market. In this third topic, we will explore the importance of adaptation to changes, strategies to identify trends, and how to cultivate a flexible mindset to thrive in the face of new challenges.

10.3.1 Importance of Adaptation:

- **Response to Emerging Trends:** Adaptation allows you to respond quickly to emerging trends. Those who can anticipate and embrace market changes have a significant competitive advantage.

- **Maintenance of Relevance:** The constant evolution of the market requires professionals to stay relevant. Those who resist stagnation and continually seek to adapt are better positioned to face challenges and seize opportunities.

10.3.2 Strategies to Identify Changes:

- **Monitoring Industry Trends:** Stay updated on industry trends through regular readings, participation in conferences, and engagement in professional communities. Understanding the environment in which you operate is crucial for adaptation.

- **Networking and Professional Connections:** Establish a strong network of professional contacts. Sharing information and insights with colleagues and mentors can provide valuable perspectives on imminent changes and emerging opportunities.

10.3.3 Cultivation of a Flexible Mindset:

- **Acceptance of Uncertainty:** Develop a mindset that accepts uncertainty as part of the process. In dynamic environments, the ability to deal with uncertain situations and adapt quickly is an essential skill.

- **Continuous Learning:** Be open to continuous learning. Be willing to acquire new skills, even if it means stepping out of your comfort zone. The constant pursuit of knowledge strengthens your adaptability.

10.3.4 Resilience and Change Management:

- **Development of Resilience:** Resilience is the ability to recover from adversity. Cultivate this skill to face challenges constructively, learn from experiences, and apply lessons learned.

- **Participation in Change Management Training:** Specific change management training can provide tools and strategies to effectively deal with transitions. This facilitates personal adaptation and positively influences teams and organizations.

10.3.5 Personal and Professional Innovation:

- **Encouragement of Creativity:** Cultivate creativity as a skill to seek innovative solutions. Be open to experimenting with new approaches and challenging the status quo, contributing to innovation in your field.

- **Controlled Experimentation:** Conduct controlled experiments in your professional practice. Test new ideas, methodologies, or strategies before implementing them on a large scale. Experimentation allows for adjustments and refinements with lower risk.

10.3.6 Monitoring the Work Environment:

- **Observation of Market Indicators:** Stay alert to market indicators such as regulatory changes, technological advancements, and consumer behaviors. This information can signal imminent changes that will affect your area of operation.

- **Continuous Evaluation of Competition:** Monitor competitors' practices and strategies. Competitive analysis provides insights into what is working and what is not, guiding adjustments to your approach.

By adopting a proactive approach to adaptation, you stay ahead of changes and contribute to shaping your professional environment.

Chapter 11

Case Studies

Practical Examples of Successful Service Providers

In chapter 11, we will explore inspiring case studies of service providers who have achieved success through innovative strategies, exceptional skills, and a dedicated approach to excellence. These practical examples offer valuable insights and lessons learned that can inspire other professionals to enhance their own practices.

Case Study 1: Sarah, Digital Marketing Consultant

Challenge: Sarah, a digital marketing consultant, faced the challenge of standing out in a saturated market. She realized the importance of specializing in a specific area to differentiate herself from the competition.

Successful Strategies:

- **Specific Niches:** Sarah chose to specialize in digital marketing for local small businesses, building a solid reputation in this niche.
- **Active Networking:** She regularly attended local events, connecting with business

owners and building a network of contacts that resulted in strategic partnerships.

- **Continuing Education:** Sarah stayed updated on the latest trends in digital marketing through online courses and certifications, ensuring that her services were always aligned with best practices.

Outcome: Sarah gained a loyal client base and saw her business grow as she became a reference in digital marketing for local small businesses.

Case Study 2: David, Freelance Software Developer

Challenge: David, a freelance software developer, faced the challenge of ensuring a steady flow of projects and clients.

Successful Strategies:

- **Strong Online Presence:** He created a detailed online portfolio, highlighting previous projects, client testimonials, and his technical skills.

- **Collaboration on Freelancer Platforms:** David used freelancer platforms like Upwork and Freelancer to find additional projects and build his reputation.

- **Professional Networking:** He actively participated in online developer communities, exchanging knowledge, receiving feedback, and occasionally receiving referrals from other professionals.

Outcome: David established a solid reputation as a freelancer, with a diverse client base. His success also led to opportunities for more complex and well-paid projects.

Case Study 3: Emily, Personal Development Coach

Challenge: Emily, a personal development coach, faced the challenge of building a successful coaching practice in a highly competitive market.

Successful Strategies:

- **Personal Branding:** She invested in developing her personal brand, creating a professional website, participating in podcasts, and writing articles on personal development.

- **Specialized Coaching Programs:** Emily developed specialized coaching programs to serve specific audiences, such as professionals in career transition and aspiring entrepreneurs.

- **Collaboration with Other Coaches:** She established partnerships with other coaches to offer workshops and joint events, expanding her visibility in the market.

Outcome: Emily built a solid coaching practice, attracting clients through her online presence, specialized programs, and strategic collaborations.

These case studies illustrate the diversity of approaches that successful service providers adopt to achieve success in their respective fields. In the next chapter, we will discuss the importance of ethics in service delivery and how it contributes to building a lasting reputation.

Chapter 12

Ethics in Service Delivery and Its Contribution to Building a Lasting Reputation

Ethics plays a fundamental role in service delivery, as it directly influences how professionals interact with clients, handle challenges, and conduct their businesses. Here are some key points about ethics in service delivery and how it contributes to building a lasting reputation:

1. **Transparency and Honesty:**
    - Transparency and honesty are essential ethical principles. Service providers should be transparent about their processes, prices, and policies, providing clear and accurate information to clients.

2. **Integrity in Customer Relations:**
    - Maintaining integrity in customer relations is crucial. This includes keeping promises, respecting deadlines, and ensuring the quality of service provided, even when no one is watching.

3. **Respect for Confidentiality and Privacy:**
    - Respecting the confidentiality and privacy of client information is

crucial. Service providers should protect confidential data and use this information only for purposes agreed upon with the client.

4. **Fairness and Justice:**

    - Fairness and justice should guide the decisions and actions of service providers. This means treating all clients fairly and impartially, regardless of their background, status, or identity.

5. **Social and Environmental Responsibility:**

    - Service providers have a responsibility to consider the social and environmental impact of their operations. This includes adopting sustainable practices, promoting diversity and inclusion, and contributing to the well-being of the community.

6. **Ethical Management of Conflicts of Interest:**

    - Service providers should manage conflicts of interest ethically, prioritizing the interests of clients and avoiding situations where their personal interests may compromise impartiality or objectivity.

7. **Clear and Open Communication:**

    - Clear and open communication is essential for establishing and maintaining trust with clients. Service providers should communicate honestly and transparently, avoiding misleading or ambiguous information.

8. **Learning from Mistakes and Taking Responsibility:**

    - Recognizing mistakes and taking responsibility for them is an important part of ethics in service delivery. Service providers should be willing to learn from mistakes and take steps to correct them and prevent them from happening again.

Building a Lasting Reputation:

- By adopting an ethical approach to service delivery, professionals build a solid and lasting reputation. Client trust is earned over time through consistent actions and ethical behavior.

- A positive reputation based on ethics not only attracts new clients but also promotes loyalty and positive word-of-mouth. Clients value service providers who demonstrate integrity, responsibility, and respect.

- Additionally, an ethical reputation strengthens relationships with clients, resulting in long-term partnerships and positive referrals. Clients trust service providers who demonstrate a commitment to ethics and social responsibility.

In summary, ethics in service delivery is not just a matter of compliance with norms and regulations but rather an imperative for sustainable success. By prioritizing ethics in all interactions and decisions, service providers build a solid foundation for a lasting reputation and mutually beneficial business relationships.

The Importance of a "Good Name"

Service providers are central figures in any sector, responsible for delivering solutions and meeting clients' needs. However, beyond providing quality service, it's crucial for the provider to safeguard their good name and reputation. A service provider's reputation is a valuable asset, built over time through consistent actions and ethical behavior. It's this reputation that influences client trust, loyalty, and business growth.

By basing their actions on solid ethical principles, service providers demonstrate their commitment to high standards of professional conduct. Ethics form the foundation upon which all interactions and business transactions should be built. It guides the provider's decisions, ensuring they do what is right, even when no one is watching. This integrity is crucial for maintaining client trust and preserving the service provider's reputation.

Ethics in service delivery goes beyond simply complying with laws and regulations. It involves acting fairly, honestly, and responsibly in all situations. This includes being transparent with clients, respecting their privacy and confidentiality, and fulfilling commitments made. When a service provider operates based on these ethical principles, they build a solid foundation for long-term relationships with clients.

A reputation tainted by unethical practices can have devastating repercussions for the service provider. Loss of client trust can lead to loss of business and future opportunities. Additionally, a poor reputation can spread quickly through negative word-of-mouth and social media, affecting the provider's credibility and their ability to compete in the market.

On the other hand, a good name based on ethics can be a powerful competitive advantage. Clients value service providers who demonstrate integrity, reliability, and commitment to their well-being. A positive reputation can attract new clients, generate referrals, and strengthen bonds with existing clients. It's a virtuous cycle where ethics fuel reputation and reputation reinforces ethics.

Furthermore, ethics in service delivery contributes to the long-term sustainability of the business. Service providers who operate ethically tend to avoid legal issues, litigation, and damage to the company's image. They are also better positioned to face challenges and crises, as they have the trust and support of their clients and communities.

Therefore, it's in every service provider's interest to safeguard their good name and act with integrity in all areas of their operation. Ethics is not only a moral obligation but also a smart strategy for long-term success. By building and preserving an ethical reputation, the service provider establishes the groundwork for lasting relationships, sustainable growth, and continuous prosperity.

Conclusion

Recap of Key Points

In the final chapter, it is crucial to recap the key points discussed throughout this manual, providing a comprehensive overview and highlighting the main lessons learned. Let's revisit the essential elements that have been explored to strengthen the understanding and preparation of the service provider.

Continuous Professional Development:

- Continuous education is essential to stay updated and relevant in a dynamic market.

- Participating in events, workshops, and seeking certifications are fundamental strategies for professional development.

Adaptation to Market Changes:

- Adaptation capability is crucial to facing challenges and seizing opportunities in the ever-evolving business environment.

- Identifying trends, cultivating a flexible mindset, and managing changes are key elements for effective adaptation.

Inspiring Case Studies:

- Practical examples of successful service providers highlight the importance of specific strategies such as specialization, networking, online presence, and strategic collaborations.

- The diversity of approaches demonstrates that there is no single recipe for success but rather the need to adapt strategies to individual realities.

Ethics in Service Provision:

- Integrity and ethics are fundamental to building a solid and sustainable reputation.
- Making ethical decisions contributes to client trust, loyalty, and sustainable business growth.

Work-Life Balance:

- Pursuing a healthy work-life balance is crucial for mental health, professional satisfaction, and consistent performance.

Legal and Contractual Considerations:

- Understanding legal forms, necessary licenses, and contract drafting is essential for establishing and protecting a service business.

Personal Branding and Client Management:

- Building a strong personal brand, using effective marketing strategies, and enhancing client management skills are key elements for success in service provision.

Best Practices in Service Delivery:

- Drafting solid contracts, efficiently managing projects, and prioritizing quality in service delivery are best practices that contribute to long-term success.

Legal and Contractual Aspects:

- Knowing rights and obligations, resolving disputes effectively, and staying updated on legal aspects are essential components for the legal security of the service provider.

Tools and Useful Resources:

- Utilizing management software, online marketing platforms, and networking resources are strategies to optimize operations and promote business growth.

Final Recap:

- The combination of continuous learning, proactive adaptation, ethical practices, work-life balance, and effective business strategy implementation forms the basis for long-term success in service provision.

By internalizing these key points, service providers will be equipped to face challenges and thrive in a dynamic professional environment. This manual serves as a comprehensive guide, but remember that success is a continuous journey of learning and improvement. Good luck on your service provision journey!

Encouragement for Continuous Success

As we come to the end of this manual, it is essential to offer words of encouragement to inspire and motivate service providers in their pursuit of continuous success. Here are some key points that can serve as a guide for a lasting and successful journey in service provision:

1. **Cultivate a Learning Mindset:**

    - Approach every challenge as an opportunity for learning. Stay curious and be open to new ideas and innovative approaches.

2. **Be Adaptable and Flexible:**

    - The business environment is constantly evolving. The ability to adapt to changes with flexibility is a valuable skill. See changes as opportunities for growth.

3. **Build Strong Relationships:**

    - Relationships are the foundation of success in service provision. Cultivate authentic connections, build a strong network, and invest in the development of lasting partnerships.

4. **Maintain an Ethical Approach:**
    - Ethics is the backbone of a solid reputation. Make decisions based on values, be transparent in your interactions, and maintain integrity in all transactions.

5. **Take Care of Your Well-Being:**
    - Remember that success is not only professional but also personal. Take care of your mental and physical health by maintaining a healthy work-life balance.

6. **Celebrate Achievements, Learn from Challenges:**
    - Celebrate every achievement, no matter how small. When facing challenges, see them as opportunities for growth. Each experience contributes to your development.

7. **Persistence is Key:**
    - The path to success may have its ups and downs. Persistence in the face of challenges is crucial. Keep honing your skills and strategies, even when encountering obstacles.

8. **Stay Connected to the Professional Community:**

- Be involved in your professional community. Exchange experiences, knowledge, and mutual support are essential elements for continuous growth.

9. **Innovate and Strive for Excellence:**

    - Always be in search of innovation. The pursuit of excellence, whether in service quality, customer satisfaction, or operational efficiency, is a competitive advantage.

10. **Learn from Diversity of Experiences:**

    - The diversity of experiences, whether through projects, collaborations, or interactions, is a rich source of learning. Seize opportunities to broaden your horizons.

Remember that success is a continuous journey, and every step you take contributes to your growth. Celebrating victories, learning from challenges, and continuing to refine your skills are fundamental elements for a successful career in service provision.

Thank you for following this manual, and I wish you a journey filled with achievements, professional growth, and personal satisfaction. Keep forging the path to success with dedication and passion for service provision. Good luck!

Recommended Books for Additional Resources

For a deeper immersion and a continuous source of valuable insights on your journey in service provision, we recommend reading the following books. These works offer practical perspectives, proven strategies, and inspiration to help enhance your professional skills and achieve sustainable success:

1. **"The Lean Startup" by Eric Ries:**
    - This book addresses essential principles for entrepreneurs and service providers, emphasizing the importance of continuous innovation, customer feedback, and operational efficiency.

2. **"To Sell is Human" by Daniel H. Pink:**
    - Pink explores the art of selling and how everyone, in some way, is involved in selling activities. The book offers insights into persuasion, influence, and effective communication.

3. **"Deep Work" by Cal Newport:**
    - Newport discusses the importance of deep focus in a world full of distractions. He provides strategies for maximizing productivity and achieving meaningful results.

4. **"The Power of Habit" by Charles Duhigg:**
   - Duhigg explores the power of habits and how understanding them can lead to positive changes both personally and professionally.

5. **"Atomic Habits" by James Clear:**
   - Clear explores how small changes in daily habits can lead to significant transformations. He offers practical strategies for building positive habits.

6. **"The 7 Habits of Highly Effective People" by Stephen R. Covey:**
   - Covey presents seven fundamental habits that can lead to a more effective and productive life. The principles discussed have direct applications in service provision.

7. **"Crucial Conversations" by Kerry Patterson, Joseph Grenny, Ron McMillan, and Al Switzler:**
   - This book addresses how to handle difficult and important conversations, a crucial skill in client management and conflict resolution.

8. **"Start with Why" by Simon Sinek:**
   - Sinek explores the importance of starting with "why" when communicating a vision or offering

services. He highlights emotional connection as a catalyst for success.

9. **"Mindset: The New Psychology of Success" by Carol S. Dweck:**

    - Dweck explores the fixed mindset versus the growth mindset and how the latter can positively impact performance and development.

10. **"Measure What Matters" by John Doerr:**

    - This book highlights the importance of defining and measuring key objectives to guide success in business and service provision.

These books offer a combination of theory and practice, bringing valuable insights from experts in different fields. By incorporating the lessons from these works into your professional approach, you will be better equipped to face challenges and achieve your goals in service provision. Happy reading and success on your journey!

www.ingramcontent.com/pod-product-compliance
Lightning Source LLC
Chambersburg PA
CBHW062220220526
45471CB00009B/3275